SHADOW READER

Imtiaz Dharker grew up a 'Muslim Calvinist' in a Lahori household in Glasgow, was adopted by India and married into Wales. She is an accomplished artist and video film-maker, and has published seven books with Bloodaxe, *Postcards from god* (including *Purdah*) (1997), *I Speak for the Devil* (2001), *The terrorist at my table* (2006), *Leaving Fingerprints* (2009), *Over the Moon* (2014), *Luck is the Hook* (2018) and *Shadow Reader* (2024). All her poetry collections are illustrated with her drawings, which form an integral part of the books; she is one of very few poet-artists to work in this way.

She was awarded The Queen's Gold Medal for Poetry for 2014, presented to her by HM Queen Elizabeth, has also received a Cholmondeley Award from the Society of Authors, and is a Fellow of the Royal Society of Literature. *Over the Moon* was shortlisted for the Ted Hughes Award for New Work in Poetry 2014. Her poems are on the British GCSE and A Level English syllabuses, and she reads with other poets at Poetry Live! events all over the country to more than 35,000 students a year. She has had a dozen solo exhibitions of drawings in India, London, Leeds, New York and Hong Kong. She scripts and directs films, many of them for non-government organisations in India, working in the area of shelter, education and health for women and children. In 2015 she appeared on the iconic BBC Radio 4 programme *Desert Island Discs*. In 2020 she was appointed Chancellor of Newcastle University. She lives in London.

Imtiaz Dharker

SHADOW READER

BLOODAXE BOOKS

ISBN: 978 1 78037 709 4

First published 2024 by
Bloodaxe Books Ltd,
Eastburn,
South Park,
Hexham,
Northumberland NE46 1BS.

www.bloodaxebooks.com
For further information about Bloodaxe titles
please visit our website or write to
the above address for a catalogue.

Supported using public funding by
ARTS COUNCIL
ENGLAND

Cover design: Neil Astley & Pamela Robertson-Pearce.

Printed in Great Britain by Bell & Bain Limited, Glasgow, Scotland, on
acid-free paper sourced from mills with FSC chain of custody certification.

CONTENTS

for Carol Ann

In the Year of My Death

When I was twenty-five
    the Shadow Reader said
        I would live to a ripe old age.

            He licked his finger, flicked a page
                and told me the year of my death.
                That year has arrived.

Out of the rose garden

When you come away from the rose garden
your eyes have changed colour in the rain
and the scent of attar follows you home.
You arrive in the city of pointing fingers
to keening sirens and beeping phones,
the clicking, the screens all on, and you
still have petals falling from your mouth.

You cross from corner to corner,
a fugitive in this time. Your eyes
are watercolour. In them, the city
and all its workings have been stamped
with gilt. The script blazes
over the walls of the meat market,
but the streets are brambled, thorned,

and on the illuminated borders
there are drops of blood.

Story

In the manuscript, the verses
are written on pages washed
with subtle colour,
aquamarine, coral, peach.

The artist worked with a crafty hand
and picked out this one word in blue:

hikayat, story.

On the gold-flecked page
an insect has bitten through

the edge of story.
Silverfish, I hope you swallowed
that sliver of gilt.

*

But the roses are savages
that will eat you
alive, given the chance.

*

.

They will not the body on a slab

Respect for this body

there will be an inquiry to determine

it is clear the bullet came from

there was some jostling

two sides clashing

we heard on the news

there is no clear indication

both sides weren't at fault

and everyone watching

The map of this country is made of scars

They will put the body on a slab for examination
                                                    no
out of respect for this body
                            no
there will be an inquiry to determine
                                        no
it is clear the missile came from
                                    no
there was some jostling two sides clashing
                                            no
as we heard on the news
                        no
there is no clear indication
                            no
both sides were at fault
                        no

Seen from above it looks like grief
wrapped in a shroud of dust,
but the blood has seeped so long
and deep it could be a ring of rust.

Out of respect the wounds will be
washed, inspected and sewn up
to look like a map of a country
that does not exist.

They will carry the body
as if it is a homeland they have lost
and brought to a field of poppies
to anoint and lay to rest.

On their shoulders they will carry the coffin
                                        yes
the mourners will lift their hands to honour her
                                              yes
there will be a bullet
                  yes
there will be jostling
                  yes
the body will spill out
                     yes
this is a wound opening
                     yes
this is a country being torn
                        yes
again and again and again
                       yes
a person falling apart
                  yes
and everyone watching
                  yes
did we watch this happening?
                        yes
did anyone see?

                  no

Face to face

Who is telling this? The one
who gives the gift, or the one who takes?

Can the writer be forgiven
by the one who is written?

Does the warp look back
at the one who is weaving and say,

This is not how I remember it,
not how it happened at all?

Who belongs
in this thing you are making?

The rose garden
throws away its symmetry

and lifts off the page
with a mind of its own.

The wind spreads rumours
and a new language blows in,

written in script that looks
like your heart beating.

Windows tilt to catch
the truth at a different angle.

Our shadow lies on this page,
Reader.

Your hand slides off parchment
to touch human skin.

Open the other face.
Look in.

Witness

Sometimes the truth is not a beacon
but a small flame

or only the light of a phone
falling on the face of a witness.

The Show

Colonel Blair and his Family and an Indian Ayah
by Johann Zoffany 1786

Not an ayah, you want to say, a *child*.

The portrait painter gives them
a noble version of themselves to take back home
and hang above a marble fireplace.

Husband and wife clasp hands, dead centre,
flanked by porcelain daughters. They have allowed
the extra girl into the frame. They do not mind

if her clothes are frayed and mended,
washed and washed again, pounded to softness
on a stone. They think of themselves as kind

masters. She has been given a cat to hold.
On the wall is a landscape with elephant
and scenes of savage customs:

a widow on her way to a funeral pyre,
a tableau of torture. This
will be a conversation piece in Perthshire.

The child is wide-eyed, caught in a performance
that goes on for years in polite rooms
full of rustling silk.

It makes a sound like scavengers
circling in the undergrowth.

They brought glass beads

She accepted them with grace.

She brought out her best,
the almonds and sweets,
sherbet from the shop.

The children went hungry
but for the guests at her table
she brought out the best.

She was the host. She opened
her home. She gave a gift.
They made a trade.

They told the story, back home,
of people like children, bought
with glass beads

and baubles of paste.
When they told it they laughed.
They could not read

the heart of the host.
All her life she was taught
god comes like a stranger

disguised as a guest, a guest
like us at the door of the earth.

The table was laden.
Something was given,

something was taken.
She brought out her best.

Boy with a Turban

Duleep Singh in Queen Victoria's sketchbook,
dressing Prince Arthur in Indian clothes

There is a crowd standing behind him
but he is unaware, engrossed in the task
of tying a turban for this child,
tucking the blond curls in, saying,
This is what we wear, where I come from.
This is who we are.

Who we are. We stand outside the line
of vision, millions of us, day labourers
in paradise gardens, who scurry underground
so our shadows never mar the path of the king.
If we have faces, they are not drawn here.
There is no paper large enough to find

or hold us. The pages of this sketchbook
rustle like the forest they come from
and speak another language,
knowing the surge of sap and leaves
breaking through to somewhere high
and dangerous.

At sixteen he is a king without a kingdom,
kneeling beside a royal child, being painted
by a queen with a silver and sable brush.
Cobalt washes over his seas and continents,
rinses a world away behind his back,
separating him from who he is
and what he could have been.

Letters home

Through steam and woodsmoke
the train slides in.

The boys who stood straight as sugar cane
have come back changed, spilled

out of carriages, still
wearing the Emperor's uniform.

There are no crowds today,
no brass or beating drums;

only a sullen silence, the sidling
sideways glance, the kind of looks

that shadowed them
in England and through France.

The letters went back and forth
through the hands of spies

read by so many eyes, the words
were all used up before they arrived.

This wasn't our fight. But a fight is a fight
and we stand shoulder to shoulder.

The enemy who paid their wages
has travelled back with them

and they say the war has ended,
but what kind of peace is this

when the crop is blasted,
home a bitter kiss?

Did anyone say what happened to the girl?

There's a picture in the phone.

She is still here, in a lavish room
in her own country.

She is still the *ayah*, only the masters
are new.

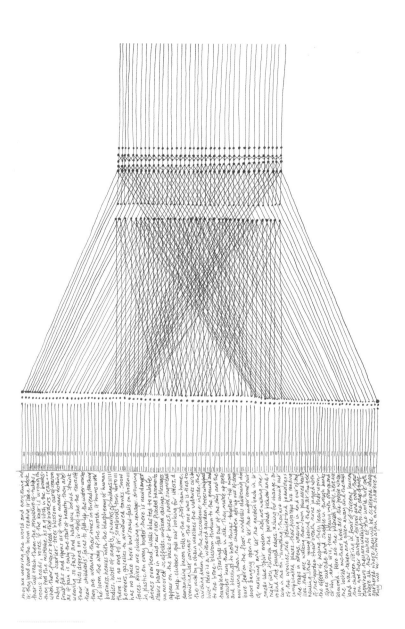

Loom

They are weaving the world and everything
that lives in it. They bend over the loom,
reading it like a book that will teach them
the structure of tulips, crocus heads, roses.
If the knot is wrong they feel the mistake
as a glitch in the bones. When their fingers
bleed the borders leak ruby and scarlet.
Trees blossom out of season, fruit fills
and ripens as if time means nothing,
as if pain is only the start of beauty.
They are weaving so hard and fast
you would think their lives depend on it.
They take the tears off their children's faces
to fill up the watercourses. They are weaving
their times in thread, teaching the loom
the way of the world. It hums with business,
heaves with the blasphemy of human bodies,
hosts of angels, swarms of midges.
There is no end to it. Songbirds turn
into bombers, gazelles to armoured tanks.
Snow has no place here but snow falls
on frozen faces. Rivers are choking in sewage,
drowning in plastic. On every border
there is a new danger, drones overhead,
walls blasted to rubble. Stairs hang
in mid-air over flooded basements,
unmoored scaffolds, unfixed railings.
Messages appear on the backs of buses,
neon signs call for help. Clubbers spill out,
looking for Ubers, demanding bacon rolls

or the first train home, vomiting at corners.
The one who is tied to the rock by a chain
watches the vultures circling down
for the succulence inside, the liver. Here
is a withered garden, trees whipped to the bone.
Starlings fall out of the sky and the weavers
bury them in the silk. They make up spells
and blessings to hold things together till morning
when the children get up out of sleep, bare feet
on the floor, windows clattering, doors banging open
to let the green back in. It smells like split melon.

The weaver makes a pitch

This is the work of many hands.

It contains all of Paradise,
eaten by moths in one small corner.

For you, special price.

This is not a prayer mat
It is the prayer
prayer
prayer
prayer
prayer
prayer
prayer
prayer
prayer
prayer
prayer
prayer
prayer
prayer
prayer
prayer
prayer
prayer
prayer
prayer
prayer
prayer
prayer
prayer
prayer

*

This is not a prayer mat.

It is the prayer.

*

Shadow Reader

Midday, and we are climbing the stairs
from Perfect Electronix and Electric Dreamz
to the second floor in one of those buildings
that had a life before it was painted pistachio
green, blistered by time and salt off the sea.

Bunches of wires swagger up the stairwell,
wagging a finger, ready to coil and drag
me up if I falter. I don't want to know
my future. All I want is to turn around
and walk away down Chowpatty beach,

along the shore where the coconut sellers
and paper windmills are, but these are early days.
when I still give in to other people's whims,
so here I am standing at a spidered door,
waiting to meet the Shadow Reader.

The weaver tells the spell

If you stick your head in the mortar
why blame the pestle?

If your hand is broken
why point at the shuttle?

Ask, I will tell. Here is a spell
that will lift the curse
if you follow the ritual,
guaranteed to ward off
the evil eye and make all well.
The demon eating the earth
from inside out will lose
its teeth, swallow a nettle.
Enemies hurtling to battle
will stop and settle
their griefs and grievances,
untangle old grudges.

Take a hair from one head,
a flake of skin or follicle
or hangnail from the other,
add the scale of a snake,
a black crow feather.
Bind them together
with a thread from the loom,
weave it in to the pile.
Singe the end of the hair.
Let it smoulder
and sleep on its anger.

By next morning
the enemies will be close
as brother or sister.

This cannot fail

unless their mothers have spat in the well,
unless their fathers have harboured the haters.

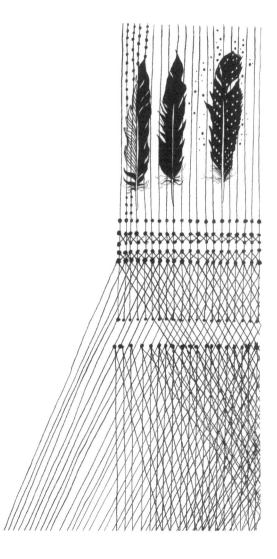

40

Demons Rule

After the folios of Prahlada from the Bhagavata Purana

How clever the demons think they are,
how quick. Where you expect

courtiers and grand viziers in the durbar
there are monsters instead,

hybrid creatures strutting among the arches
and colonnades, dressed to kill,

with heads of beasts, clawed, fanged, grotesque
and completely ridiculous.

You can wash as much as you like
but a fly will still sit on your face.

Above them all sits the demon king,
accepting homage from his conquered enemies,

the lucky survivors, the lackeys, all bowing
to him; everyone but the one rebel.

The demons know all there is to know
about manipulating the media, fiddling the feed.

They have their knobbly fingers in every game.
It should be child's play for them

to rid the ruler of the one who defies him.
They throw him in a well,

over a cliff. He comes back. They try
poison in the food, a venomous snake. No effect.

They scratch their heads, find lice. They send
an elephant to trample him to death. Not a scratch.

Dig a grave for me
and I will bury you in it.

It is a long story, so long the hill artists
started telling it centuries ago

and it still goes on. But look
at the demons' faces, perplexed.

Plot after plot, frustrated. One by one
disgraced, sacked, retired, fired, sent off

the programme with their Samsonite bags
and their tails between their legs,

saying, *They just didn't get my passion.*
The Pahari artists should be here today

to paint them with their hairy backs
and rictus grins, along with the demon king

who believes with every bone in his body
that he cannot be dislodged.

As I said, it is a long story.

What goes of your father?

Surpanakha, the demon's sister, spits

So! I am too forward, too loose,
full-mouth make-up, rusted hair,
bells and rings on my toes, tattoo
too well-placed, too in your face,
double body, single clothes. What goes?
Tell! What goes of your father?

So, I am not one of these but maybe
one of those? My demon brother has ten heads
and twenty hands, but I am under no man's
thumb, out of control of fatherbrotheruncleson,
queening and loafing in my forest alone.
What goes, eh? What goes of your father?

So? Not pure, not demure, not shy,
I choose to be too much, too much myself,
out of bounds for you. Admit you liked it, no?
Unzipped your halo? Your holiness slipped?
Brave hero! Comecome! Cut off
my ears my nipples my nose. What goes?

So who is to judge, whose the sin?
I will change shape, grow myself back again.
Sharpen my wits to match my nails,
spit on my hands, slap my thighs.

Let the battle begin.

Fly

The Decapitation, Padshanama

Such beauty. You will stop in your tracks
when you see how the bodies interlock
in the dance that happens after war,
remade in art.

Your eyes will be drawn
to the warriors' victorious strut,
the embellishments, the lovingly rendered
gleam and puff of armour, trappings,

button, cuff; the symmetry
of horses' necks, the way they arch,
the downward dip of heads,
pointing to where I am

busy. My coming and going makes
a crown around this severed head,
a lacy ruff around the neck, honeyed
with enemy blood, and all is good.

The artifice! A chinar bends
above the scene, watchers ranged
under a gold-leaf-sky, hair meticulous,
hands most delicately placed,

every human face serene.
Only the grotesques recoil as if
they have been forced
to witness something obscene.

Today the enemy's head lies here;
the victor's head another year, and threading
it all together is my lazy flight. I wind
and weave at the centre of this carnival,

gorgeous, engorged. My buzzing
is the music that reminds you
of something you always knew,
staring you in the ears:

on every flowered field
where the beloved lies, I am the one
who delivers the final delirious kiss
and says the last goodbyes.

I Am Not Alone

A line of ants climbs with me
to the Shadow Reader's door.
One ant moves forward, another
takes its place. Its shadow draws
a map of the journey it has made,
hauling the weight of the world
through the long light of morning.

In the house of an ant
there is always mourning.
There must be a scroll
somewhere that tells its life
and future, its daily battles,
its presence on the stairs, the way
it barely stirs the air and one day

disappears.

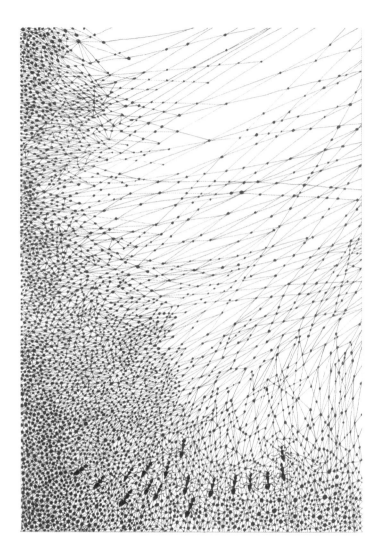

48

The Shadow Reader Is Measuring

He whips out a notched ruler and mumbles
numbers on to a tattered square-lined jotter,
adds, subtracts, reaches up behind his head
without looking back, pulls out a scroll and
reads. He shakes his head, sucks his teeth.
The shadow unrolls, dissolves and starts to seep
into the cracks where the linoleum is missing
or scratched. It goes from black to purple,
becomes detached, swims away from my feet,
changes to fish, ant, elephant, continent,
writes itself in five languages, ten scripts,
grows wings. It is Gilgamesh, Mahabharat, epic.
It belongs to the soil and the air. It never looks back.

Saying No

Even at twenty-five
   I could do without astrologers
      telling me what I should not do.

         But that was before I learned the art
        of saying *No*. No one
         knew how much I didn't

             want to go. So here I am, stuck
            with the Shadow Reader's
             long-term headfuck.

Pink

They came along one day and planted
a flag on the cheek of the earth.

Here is the Truth, they said, *And we own it.*
The Truth had a pink skin like a child's balloon

at a birthday party and everyone had to sing
Happy Birthday and *God Save the King*.

This went on quite a long time, the singing,
the skin stretching, stretching over the Truth

till you could see right through
to its nothing.

Every child knows a balloon has to burst
or run out of breath.

When the skin splits,
truth is the thing that smells like red earth

and sounds like the silence
before the pouring rain.

Chori

They are just asking to be taken,
shouting to be shaken out of the tree
in the neighbours' garden.

If you do it, what would you call it?
Scrumping, poaching,
chori?

The big boy next door can see you.
He has a black smear of hair and a scar
on one eyebrow.

His mother is huffing and tutting,
saying *What do you expect, it's
those children*

and he has an Alsatian,
so it's only a wish you make
under your breath

while the sky steals fistfuls of light
and keeps it up there, gloating
in the gloaming when it should be night.

Where things belong and who they belong to.

Midges draw crowns on your head. You
are monarch of the shrubs and trees
and all their blue shadows inside your borders.

The plums hanging over the wall are your
birth right, heavy with promise. The juice
doesn't ask permission to live in the fruit.

Where things begin and what they grow into,

dangled into your queendom.
When their time comes, they fall for you.
You hear their hearts thumping.

Where you belong

You can squat in this room if you don't say a word,
you can stay in this town if you pay for a room,
you can go on this train if it's off-peak,
you can speak your mind if you change your look,
you can have your chance if you don't expect luck,
you can be in the group if you get enough likes,
you can live with family if you toe the line,
you can keep your children if we countersign,
you can enter this church if you quote the book,
you can open the book if you close your mind,
you can save our time if you follow the rules,
you can play a role if you buy the mask,
you can take on the task if no one else wants it,
you can ask the question if you never offend,
you can belong but only if you don't stay too long,
you can end it now or start over again,
you can follow the signs but never turn back,
you can see you have run out of time and years,
you can leave in tears or go with a laugh,
you can take your clothes but leave your shoes and
your attitude behind, it does you no favours, and
you can do us a favour, don't change your mind.

What it grows into

It's for all the slights, the casual put-downs,
the sideways swipes, being overlooked
and underpaid, laid and ghosted,

missing the grade, not being sure
if you'd phrased it right
or wrong or if you were to blame.

It was losing the fight
at every street corner, being questioned
at every border, stopped and searched,

dumped on and dangled, called exotic,
hysterical, hormonal, foreign, neurotic.
You could have crawled in a hole but instead

you trawled the net, browsing fish whacks,
baseball bats, and discovered this slugger
that arrived overpacked in the post.

You think about it sometimes, stashed
in the wardrobe, still bubble-wrapped,
next to the wellies, under the coats.

Back

When the person holding your passport says,
You'll have to go back where you came from,
you are four again, crossing the bridge at Jamaica
Street, the River Clyde rolling under your feet
away to the sea where ships set sail;

and when the woman in the queue mutters
This is not where you belong, you think of
the way light plays hide-and-seek
over the hills on the Sunday morning ride
up the Campsie Fells;

and when the man outside the pub looks you up
and down and says, *Go back to your country,*
you know you could squash the stoater,
if you could be bothered, with *Go back
to yer cave and bile yer heid, ye dolly walloper!*

and even if you're wired to the moon,
that's when your heart goes home and you
coorie doon, all of Glasgow shining in your window,
because this is where you came from,
the place that will always have your back.

Redeem

To see this stone as it wants to be seen,
forget the colour

of the skin, scarred
and weathered to the bone.

In a trick of scale,
the man of god looms over

a diminished man and woman,
their bodies smoothed out, childlike.

Stone can learn
to be sentimental.

Marble can be taught
to kneel.

If you turn away,
the hovering

hand becomes a bird of prey, poised
to swoop on souls that must be saved,

children of god
set in stone, the stone enslaved.

If you choose to turn
and look again

at the lifted hand, knowing no man
can make you kneel,

even this stone might raise its head
and feel

redeemed.

*

When you hear the wind
and think it is your own voice
howling, find this space.

*

The welcome

You were running on broken glass,
a child chased by nightmares
down battered streets, until at last
you came to this door. Here

are rooms made of hope, shelves full
of voices that call you in. They say
you can stop running now, pull
out a chair and sit. For you, they lay

a table with a feast that tastes of places
in your dreams, honey from the hive,
warm bread, words like spices.
This is where people come alive

to speak their stories in ink and blood
on wild nights, dappled afternoons,
telling of fallen tyrants, drought and flood
under desert stars and arctic moons.

They spin legends and conjure myths
in mother tongues and other tongues
that give your accent to their dance with death,
their love of life, the songs they sing.

You have been welcomed in
to books that smell like ancient trees,
standing here with broken spines,
opening like thoughts set free

and as the pages turn, your breath
quickens with something you always knew
in your blood like remembered faith.
When you open the book, it opens you.

The key

The room is holding itself close
like the hush when you know
it will snow or the sky goes yellow
before a monsoon rain starts falling.

You sit in a corner on the floor
where bookshelves meet
and find that the span of your arms
can hold a continent or more.

Even if you have no country
that would claim you,
no handful of mud to call your own
or home you want to go to,

this could be yours.
Language starts to crack
the way an egg hatches
and a beak appears.

You feel the heat
of the earth waiting for rain,
trees in the forest, bending
to the wind, see the life

of the woman on the train. You hear
what the books are saying.
You are the key.
You turn. The world opens.

Reader

You come to the books
to take you away, but they
open to welcome you home
and you stay.

The piece

Mammy, throw us doon a piece.
Tossed from the third floor window, caught
before it hits the pavement, no time lost.
She can do without a troop of neighbourhood
children tramping through the close
and up her new-washed stairs with filthy feet,

and anyway, what would a monkey know
about the taste of ginger?

Only if the catch is missed, it lands
like a massacre on the tar macadam, paper split,
white bread and jam streaked red. There's pelting
up and down the street till lamps are lit,
Ma heid's bleedin, ma face is cut
Kiltie kiltie cauld bum, three stairs up.

You come back bloodied from the turf wars,
Protestant against Catholic,
Rangers against Celtic,
and never think to say, *This isn't our fight.*
A fight is a fight. You stand shoulder to shoulder
by the middens. It feels right,

even when you make it to the close
with a knocked-out tooth or a bloody nose,
ready for her tongue-lashing,
Why stick your nose in?
What goes of your father?
before you get to wolf down a piece

of the other country, the hot tukra
and ginger with the sting of Punjab
in the tail.

For the Minicab Driver Who Looked as if He Needed Feeding

He looks so young, his hands
bony at the wheel. I wonder
if he has been out all night, what
he might have had for breakfast
and what he eats when his shift ends;
whether his mother makes him
Punjabi samosas or Bengali mustard fish
or Kerala rice, if he prefers
the mangoes of the north, like me,
or the sweeter ones from further south.
Before I can stop them, the words
fall out of my mouth, *And where
are you from... I mean,
your people?* They land somewhere
on the back of his neck, slide into the rear-
view mirror, roll into his eyes.
He looks back for one second
and his face is a passport
and his back is a flag
and he says, Barnsley,
and I pay, and get out.

For the Woman Who Will Bring Biryani Next Time

Doctors these days. This one is a bacha,
twelve years old. What will he understand
of this lumbering body with its pain on the left
and its groan on the right and everything creaking
like my father's bullock-cart in between?

He looks ready to drop. He has tapped
and listened to twenty-two bodies today, every
age and colour, the whole of the morning queue.
I have to pull up my kameez and undo
the pyjama but it doesn't matter,

I'm old enough to be his grandmother
and there is nothing here he hasn't seen.
Breathe out, he says, and his hands
are on the belly, going after the quarry,
Just palpating the liver.

I think of my mother folding me up
in her big body, holding me
to her heart, but she would say *liver,*
kaleja, the place where love lives.
You are my liver, she says,

and this doctor-child is holding my liver
through folds of flesh and skin.
How long has it been since anyone
touched this thing as if it was precious,
as if it was the Koh-i-Noor?

For the Girl on the Elizabeth Line

Standing by the door
the way young people do,
as if a seat is a waste
of life, you are lost

in each other. His hand
in your hair, he is speaking softly
into your ear. You stand
quite still, head down, listening,

then your face begins
to do that terrible thing where
it looks like paper being crumpled
before it is thrown away

because the poem doesn't work
and the page is cruel. In another
life, you would shake his hand
off your neck

and know how it feels
to be touched with respect

but the doors open at Tottenham
Court Road and he steers you out
with the flat of his hand on your back
and the people in the carriage

try not to look at each other.

For the Woman Who Changed Back to a Snake

You never needed those coils of pearls
to lend you brilliance, your body jewelled
at birth by me. No ivory or opals could match
your sinewed geometry. Cruel,

this human love that twists and flails, fails
and eats itself. If only he had seen
you were akin, or followed the trace of scales
from his own forked body to your perfect sheen.

They can say you vanished. You made the choice
to fall into the earth's waiting arms
and find the tongue you lost, your silenced voice,
away from man's narrow gaze and casual harm,

back to the place that calls you goddess, queen,
and shivers at the power of your skin.

Cross

Stop in the space between criss and cross.
The North East light shears in

and divides your face. Slices of sky and Tyne
fall through the angles cut out of time

and time looks like nothing,
from where you are, but a feat of engineering,

riveted to the moon, held up by belief.
Lean in and the minutes flicker, seconds flare.

A hum begins down in the girders and climbs
the ribs like a thief, swings on horizontals,

skims up verticals, steals all the stripes in the world
and wants more: the living thing that slithers between.

It takes calligraphy off the wall of a mosque
and rewrites it as music; recalibrates the geometry

of presence and loss.
                    Close your eyes.

Behind the lids you still own the span of line on line
and time that stretches over a borderline.

The dazzle of it.
Open your arms and run across.

So How Does This Work? I Ask

The Shadow Reader tuts.
His mouth is a purse pulled tight.

To understand the shadow,
you have to see the light.

*

A door full of light,
walls made of nothing but words.
Traveller, come in.

*

Swiping Left on Larkin

Here he is younger, his shoulders
thinner. She flicks a finger,
swipes left. He is dismissed
without a flicker.

If they pass on the street she sees
a boy trudge by with a book and satchel
under the arm, on the way to a lifetime
of drudge, easy to overlook.

In the edge of his eye she is a blur
between staying or dying,
a whiff of abroad, the chaos
of prams and infants teething.

At the end of every birth is grieving.
He takes the dark for a walk, his light
on a leash through the sputtering streets
of a town caught in the act of drowning.

From a window a curtain is waving
but his back is turned. Shops shut up
and shutters come down on the chatter
of living, the guttering years.

All roads lead to a leaving.
He goes in to the bar of the station hotel,
sits for a while. When he leaves, he leaves
a pale ring on the table. Gold

spills out of basements over his feet.
He walks down a street and out
of his name. Beyond rumour and fame,
a flurry of letters blown into gutters,

the glitter of language on cobbles,
his words remain, hard as knuckles,
bright as believing or half-believing.
At the end of the world there is always

the sea and its breathing,
swiping right, swiping right
across a blue screen
to something beginning.

Let's Meet in the Place Called Jazz

In a city you can't be bothered to love

your words drop like coins into a well
and grow back out of every hole in the wall.
I'm walking beside you, trying to keep up,
laughing because this is absurd,
me chasing you down the street,

you trying not to meet my eye.

Let's put our differences aside, even if
your mind wants to swing shut
on the ones who don't fit. While
we have the time, let's agree to meet
in the smoky room called Jazz.

Let's improvise.

In Which I Am Ghosted by William Blake

I thought it went so well, the non-stop
talk, a pint at King's Cross, the walk
to the top of Primrose Hill. I was new
to the city and he scrolled through the sights
for me, the Shard, the Eye, St Paul's,
high-rise pillars of gold. It was as if
he lifted his hand and rolled out a net
of lights at my feet. He said he wrote poems.
His hand slid to his pocket but he didn't offer
to read. I sighed with relief - but I did like
hearing him speak, watching his mouth,
how fast it moved, and his ink-
spattered hands.

We had a laugh. He knew how to amuse
and even asked me about myself.
It felt *real*. I did notice he lost track,
once or twice, while I was speaking.
His eyes wandered off as if
he had seen something I couldn't see

in the trees.

He didn't seem to care that I called him
a bit of a geek. Or maybe he did.

I got over it of course. Last week
I stopped waiting for the beep

on the phone and his name
to come up on the screen.

He wasn't the first to do it but
there was something about this one.

Sparky. That's what he was.

Here's my final message, the last try:

Yo! Are you sick?

No reply.

I Find Faiz Blowing on His Saucer of Tea

I find Faiz blowing on his saucer of tea
at the corner café.
Faiz-Uncle, I say, *You wouldn't recognise*
our old neighbourhood.

The landlord raised the rent
and all the people we knew are gone.

Your garden has been left to die in the drought.

Someone has taken your books off the shelves
and printed them again without the words.

The koels have been rounded up and put in cages.

The singers who sang your songs have been
strangled in front of a live studio audience.

Faiz picks up the saucer and drinks from it.

When the heart is full it makes a tear
on the face of the earth.

You call it grief.
I say it is hope of a flower.

I think this is what he said but
I could be mistaken.

His words might have been
garbled in translation.

80

Away

The child is jumping as high as she can on the bed.
Thursday light makes X-rays of her feet.

She is singing in time
to the springs, creak down, bounce up.

The windows are still there.
In the time of waiting there is

embarrassment. All that expectation
and nothing

happens. They go to coffee shops, buy
baby buggies, have their hair trimmed.

The morning unfolds out of a clear sky
and brings a sound so shy at first they hardly think

they need to hide. Shadows are erasures,
crossing out the day before, what they did

and who they were. The front door
is blotted out. Outside

in the street the dead will be uncollected.
All she will remember of this time

is the light and the song.
She wriggles when they try to hold her.

When she wonders about the thunder
on this cloudless day, they gather her up.

When she asks *Where are we going?*
they say *Away.*

There are no words

They turn on sheets of dust
towards the smoother, cooler edge

of sleep. The sky
has knotted itself into grey questions

and the children are quiet. A newspaper
from a time when there was news

flaps past the shut-up shops,
down the wordless street.

*

They travel over rough terrain,
tunnels swallow them and spit them out again.

A lost part of them stays in the dark,
hoping that in time someone will explain

how they can leave what they are leaving behind,
where they are going, what they hope to find.

Next

It could come through the letterbox
on a rag soaked in kerosene. It could
be the sound of a window smashed in,
the rush of petrol poured under the door,
fingers of liquid reaching for skin.

You will try to forget the smell of burning flesh.
You will not ask what happens next.

For the girl whose hair escaped

The things that can happen
in the back of the van.
The culprit can be just sitting there
and out of nowhere the jaw
comes apart and the teeth
are lying on the floor.
Amazing, if you think
about it. Next thing you know
she is lying against the door
with cracked ribs, the air
squeezed out of her lungs.
It's a wonder, the way
she picks up her body, all
the broken bones, climbs
to the top of the precinct roof
and throws herself off.
You wouldn't believe it
but here it is in the Report,
in black and white

white as white
as the light she escapes to,
black as black
as her rampant hair.

What it is like

It's like rummaging around your life
wondering what you can sell
to keep things going.

It's like gathering every precious thing,
every necklace and nose ring you own,

begging for reluctant favours,
calling in the outstanding loans.

It's like taking a glass trinket
to an emperor who wears
your father's emeralds on his head.

It's like making a begging bowl
of your hands to hold the salty love
you have in your heart;

like collecting it, grain by grain,
and travelling across deserts
to give a handful of salt back to the sea.

What you can buy with a bangle

Pure soft gold, twenty-four carats.

It buys a way out but not the way back.

It buys a daily wage, a pay-packet.

It takes the target off her back.

It doesn't buy a lock on the door.

It doesn't buy a life-jacket.

Naa Ja

Look, it's there at your fingertip.
When you stand at the edge you almost believe
you could put out your hand
and touch the other side.

Don't go

Your hands are cold, transparent
in the morning light. The water is clear
as if to say its heart is pure. It will be night
by the time you reach the other side.

Naa ja

The boatman has not promised paradise
but the boat looks sound and he has taken
your coin. He spits on his hands
and turns his face to the other side.

Don't go

He doesn't care to see the bruises on your skin,
the scars of the place you are running from,
the wounds you carry with you
to the other side.

Naa ja

However

They say she buried the book
under the peach tree but it would not stay put.
First a scribbled shoot, then the stalks appeared
and spelt out the name of their god
in upright strokes that made it clear
what she had hidden. It sprouted
the tell-tale script of their language.
The garden was humming

with what she planted among the mint leaves
that flavoured her fingers and clung
to her hands. Whatever she did, she has gone
to learn a new script. The phone
rings in a hollowed house but whoever it is
at the other end of the line gives up
and the ringing stops. The peaches drop
with the sound of soft bodies.

*

Whoever was taken was due
to be processed. Whatever was said
or implied, the lie was retracted,
the question redirected. There is nothing
to see here but a woman reading, nothing
to hear but her finger moving on paper, no
harm intended.
However

it is true the body is broken.
However, the eyes are live.
The tongue remembers the hint of cumin,
peach juice splashed down the chin,
the taste of a life before
barbed womb, barred door, bared teeth
in the jaws of power.
However, the breath is butterfly.

It was the fault of the clothes

It was the fault of the summer dresses
with halter straps, glittery bodices,

shiny trainers, slippery anoraks.
They were to blame.

Born under a hideous flickering green,
they spoke the language of authority,

learned the ways of the correction facility.
The clothes did it all. They were good

at following instructions: Cut off this tongue
to fit the cloth, tear open this unruly seam,

stitch up this mouth.

Under a sick light the polyester
roses bloom and bloom.

*

Only you can tell
what roads began and ended
in your restless heart.

*

They arrive

They are curve and line
pleated into the fabric of the land

as if a hand has folded time
between the cloud and lake

to make a space for them.
They are not guests.

They have flown between seasons,
across a clock face

from dawn to evening rain,
calling each other through the storm

to reach this home.
They hold the memory

of ancestors arriving
out of another century.

Alert to the blue
dart of dragonflies,

a frog startled out of hiding
or fish sliding through water,

they live in *now* and *this*.
They know what it is

to be concentrated, still,
in the second before the kill.

Fold

We fold and fold
blank paper.

Rooms cannot hold
our anxious heart

or contain the splinters
when the breaking starts.

Outside, the ground
snarls under moving feet.

Blue light glares
along a sullen street.

A wall buckles. Chairs
and tables jolt off the floor.

Looking for home,
someone knocks at a door

and all the world
is calling, calling.

The cranes are standing
in the shallows

demanding
nothing.

They do not ask to be cast
as metaphor,

messenger, immortal,
reflection of a human need.

We are the ones who fold
and pleat and plead.

They rise above
the weight of our asking, wanting.

When they leave, their shadows make
the shape of a blessing in the quiet lake.

They leave

like words taking off
at a slant, italics written
in a language we cannot translate
but understand, blown off the page
in an upward arc.

This loop here means *go*.
This curve spells *come back*.

As they go

As they go, opening into the sky,
The world looks up to them.

This must be what a prayer looks like
when it learns to fly.

*

Take one step forward
and the light will find your face.
You are the story.

*

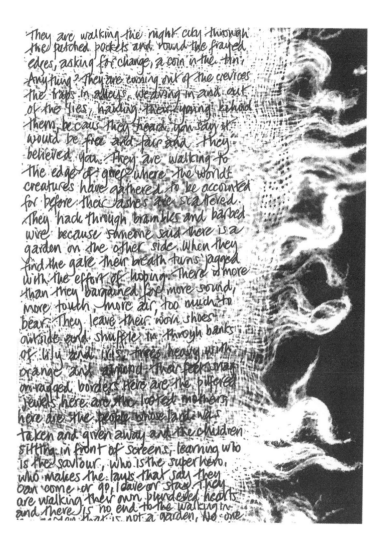

They are walking the night city through the patched pockets and round the frayed edges, asking for change, a coin in the tin, anything? They are coming out of the crevices the traps in alleys, weaving in and out of the lies, hauling their young behind them, because they heard you say it would be free and fair and they believed you. They are walking to the edge of grief where the world's creatures have gathered to be accounted for before their ashes are scattered. They hack through brambles and barbed wire because someone said there is a garden on the other side. When they find the gate their breath turns jagged with the effort of hoping. There is more than they bargained for more sound, more touch, more air, too much to bear. They leave their worn shoes outside and shuffle in through banks of lily and iris, trees heavy with orange and almond that feel mad on ragged borders. Here are the pilfered jewels here are the looted mothers, here are the people whose land was taken and given away and the children sitting in front of screens, learning who is the saviour, who is the superhero, who makes the laws that say they can come or go, leave or stay. They are walking their own plundered hearts and there is no end to the walking in a world that is not a garden. No one

102

They are walking

They are walking the night city,
through the patched pockets
and round the frayed edges, asking
for change, a coin in the tin, *Anything?*
They are coming out of the crevices,
the traps in alleys, weaving in
and out of the lies, hauling
their young behind them, because
they heard you say it would be free
and fair and they believed you.
They are walking to the edge of grief
where the world's creatures have gathered,
the horses and elephants, rabbits and pheasants
with their heads up and down, waiting
to be accounted for before their ashes
are scattered. They hack through brambles
and barbed wire because someone said
there is a garden on the other side.
When they find the gate their breath
turns jagged with the effort of hoping.
There is more than they bargained for,
more sound, more touch, more air,
too much to bear. They leave their worn
shoes outside and shuffle in through banks
of lily and iris, trees heavy with orange
and almond. Their feet snag on ragged
borders. Here are the pilfered jewels,
here are the looted mothers, here
are the people whose land was taken
and given away and the children sitting

in front of screens, learning who
is the saviour, the superhero,
who makes the laws that say
they can come or go, leave or stay.
They are walking their own plundered
hearts and there is no end to the walking
in the garden that is not a garden.
No one is watching so there is no way
to know if they are still walking, still
breathing or falling over the edge
of this poem that is not a poem.

Night Walk with Ghosts, Smithfield

By nightfall, there is blood in the streets,
moon in the blood.

The lines are drawn and drawn again
through ancient bones, the signatures
written clear as words on pages,
where they lived and when
they moved, what they ate, the hunger
they endured, the plagues that came and went
and came again.

All night, all life is here,
where the smooth fields were,
and with the meat vans, the clattering bins,
the ghosts and I, we all come in.

Night Walk with Dancing Bones

Picking up their priceless bags and walking away from the scene, whole parties of skeletons, rattling bones, are making their way over the road to the new museum, joints creaking. They don't walk in a straight line. They can't bear to go past the bars where people are drinking, but wait till dark to jiggle over the park, across Charterhouse Square where their bones were at rest. Soon they'll be on the red carpet, flocking to the galas, the fundraisers. The skeleton people will come to the ball and dance in clothes more famous than they are. Oh the organza, the outrageous billows of frills, the foam and waves and oceans of tulle, acres of satin and miles of silk all bunched and ruched and trimmed with skulls of small animals and wings of beetles. They cross the city and they keep coming back. For the shoes, the rush, the cameras, the crack.

Night Walk by the Canal

The water is slick
with the city's oils
spilt round the shape
of an egg, but the egg
is sick as the city at night.
It's all stop and search,
life and death, plastic
hatching at the edge.
A needle of wind
turns over a rusty leaf
to scan the underside
for an absent nymph.
It finds a vein.
The sky is stained
where the hawthorn
laid its head,
its bed of blossom
left unmade, a disgrace.
The dancers were graceful
but they left the floor
when their insides
heaved up in the acrid rain.
You watch the rainbowed
water as if it is a window
waiting to break, in case
they come back, diving in
and out of the sluggish
surface with that flourish
they have, the swagger,
the flash of arrival,
the bling.

Night Walk with Lit Windows

The roads are the same, but they
have pulled on a hood

that kills the sound and shadows
the walls. Windows

begin to light up. Everyone
is home, some in their rooms,

that girl in a kitchen. From a bulb
above, light falls

so hard it bleeds out her forehead
and bruises her cheek.

She is at the table checking
her phone again, again,

tapping, tapping
for word of outside.

Eyes down, she could be
praying, her prayers answered

with pictures of kittens
and dogs, a promise of kindness.

May the gods she finds at her shrine
give what she asks for

and more: stretches of coastline,
rivers and oceans with all their creatures,

orchards overflowing with apples.
Click here, post this. Please share.

She looks out of the window to where
you are. You wave. She lifts her hand.

Night Walk with Fox

It could be a river or just a rumour.
The roar falls into the meadow
under the pavement and day drains away.
Farringdon Street shakes off its cars
and changes back to the River Fleet.
From the top of the tower, woodcock
reads street as water, concrete
as cliff-face, rooftop as rock. Bats
flicker over the lake, field mice mistake
tunnels for burrows. Black
redstart comes back to the home
printed into its bones.
                              The eyes of a fox
rake the walkway for crossings.
The city's skin is porous
to those who remember with wings,
with beak and claw, radar or shoot.
London Rocket takes root in secret clay,
ragwort stows away on a trading ship,
travels up from the docks, follows
rail tracks to the City.
Shut down the earth, burn it or bomb it,
poison it, churn it, it keeps opening
its heart. It grows itself back
with seeds that unlock
fennel, nettle, camomile, dock.

Night Walk with Blackbird

Night Walk is long as the dark,
dark long as the shadow,
shadow long as lost gods,
gods long-gone as gutted words.

Because I have walked so many miles alone,
because it has been too long since I saw your face,
the rings are falling off my fingers,
bangles sliding off my wrists.

When I come to count the dead
they do not look like numbers.
They look like people who were loved,
laid with care on hospital beds.

Over the long wailing of ambulances,
a blackbird begins to sing
and I think, *This is what I mean. This
is what I was trying to say all along.*

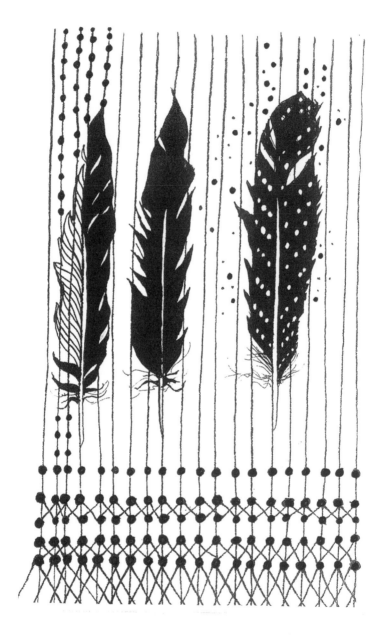

Night Walk with Voices

They come uninvited,
from a place outside,
past the divide, born in a district
you have never visited.

Off the street, the crazy
paving, out of cracks
alive with ants and roots,
the bruises of old songs.

Caught in the throat,
you could mistake them
for a winter cough. They are
nothing but hinges

that allow the door to swing
open for the unexpected
stranger who brings word
from paradise.

They croak from cramped
corners, from distances
that cannot be measured.
The voices are speaking

over each other, praying
for impossible things.
They will cause turbulence
but no masks will fall

from overhead, only black
feathers. They are a want,
a need that nothing can feed.
They are a wound

that can never be bandaged.
They are a waste
that nothing can salvage.
You will crave their body

though they are unbodied,
They will caress you and leave you
battered and bloodied.
You will chase them and know

you are the hunted.
If you close your ears
and try not to hear them
you still have them inside you.
You are the haunted.

Cranes lean in

Cranes lean in, waiting for an all-clear
that will not come.

Forehead pressed to glass,
phone at my ear, I learn

to sail on your voice
over a sadness of building sites,

past King's Cross, St Pancras,
to the place where you are.

You say nothing
is too far, mothers

will find their daughters,
strangers will be neighbours,

even saviours
will have names.

You are all flame
in a red dress.

Petals brush my face.
You say at last

the cherry blossom
has arrived

as if that is what
we were really waiting for.

Seen from a drone, Delhi

People standing in windows,

sauntering out of houses
loaded with bags and boxes, laptops,
iPads, kindles and chargers, hairdryers,
olives, chocolates, children, skeleton
staff, one maid and driver,
wending their way up vacant roads
to the place in the hills, the nearest
neighbour far over the valley,
out in the orchards, under the awnings
and yellow umbrellas. There they are
waving, there they are yawning.

Here are the rats behind tinted windows,
leaving in convoys, consulting watches
and phones, all flashing lights, bullish
horns, outriders in sunglasses powering
through, scattering these people who never
will learn to keep their distance, who never
hear the warnings, herd together like cattle,
these jostlers, these fruit-sellers, vendors,
dress-makers, cobblers, tea-boys and hawkers,
these cleaners, day-labourers, fetchers
and carriers, these unskilled workers.

These people, these people, ants
in an anthill, down there running
this way and that, carrying bundles of rags,
bundles of bundles that cry like babies,

swarming on buses and trains. Stopped.
The drone is recording: grandmothers,
mothers and fathers, daughters and sons
heaving burdens, holding each other
up, holding each other, illegally touching
gathering thronging clustering clutching
starting the long walk home.

The eye of the drone watches them going.

Gone.

Seen from a drone, Mumbai

On Day 5, look how our city is beautified
by the absence of these people. Clarified
totally, hushed. No chaos now or crowds.
Witness this historic moment, sights
you would never have thought to see
in your lifetime. Here is a bird's-eye
view of the unburdened flyover, cricket-
less stadium, unpeopled shore.
By Permission of the Authorities, we
are empowered to bring, direct
to your smartphone, these unprecedented
scenic Scenes from a Drone. Feast
your eyes on the Throne of Power,
the House of State Government,
Office of Police Commissioner, this
place of worship, its saffron flag. See
the sea-link snaking over sea, trains
like maggots feeding on carcass
of station. So much silence, deafening.
Our sound track is fitting, one
long drone broken only by birds
disturbed, on a spiral
up to the camera. Then birdsong.
Even in Lockdown there is a Moral
to be found. Nature Triumphs.
This is what the tweets are saying.
Dolphins in Venice went viral,
no matter it was a hoax,
fish were revealed in the canal
and in Llandudno the goats

ran wild and joyful in the streets.
This is truly happening
all over Twitter, all over
the whole world.

Seen from a drone

All simplified.
Some live, some die,
some rage, some stop,
some clutch their baggage closer,
others drop all they are holding
and, empty-handed,
walk on.

On mute

There is a video recording
of the incident.

Here is a woman on the station platform.
She is lying down. Her face is covered.

Her face is covered with a rag
or it could be clothing.

She is lying still.
There are people standing around her

some with phones. No one
is touching her.

There is a child holding
a corner of her clothing.

The child is crying.
The tears look real.

There is a child who could be crying
but there is no sound.

One says this, another says that

Maybe the truth happened
before the video started
or after the clip ended.
Maybe it was nipping at the heels
of the person who posted,

but looking at the comments,
there's another point of view.
The incident took place two years ago.
She did not die.
She is still alive in another city.

She made it through. The culprit
caught on camera has apologised
for any offence that might
have been caused
inadvertently.

There is a slippage
on cobbled words and canted stage.
If you don't pay attention
the sense slides off the page.

This one is sitting on the fence,
that one says there are always two sides.
They say it is old truth,
chewed over, spat out, used up,

stale news.

X

Hand shaking on the stopcock, she looks
at the X, the warning cross,

the water-tap unlocked, its padlock cracked.
Breath hacks in the throat, Check your back.

Turn it on and an anxious mutter swells
to thunder in the plastic bucket. *Don't spill it.*

Fill it to the top. Lift to the hip, stop,
balance the weight for the dangerous walk

home. *Home.*
Don't lose a drop.

From the police post across the track
a whistle, a shout. *Run. Don't stop. Don't slip.*

A drag at the hip. *Hot, hot* underfoot. Water slops
up and out in every direction, over the lip,

over her legs, a shock of cool, a spark of light.
With her stolen piece of sky, she has taken flight.

Behind her, the shouters give up. She puts down
the bucket. The water stills.

She looks into it, looks up to where the blue
is scarred with aimless tracks.

Jet-trails cross each other off
before they die out, a careless X.

*

Life chases your feet,
leaving a ribbon of light
wherever you walk.

*

Sweeping

It begins as a wave lapping over
the pebbles of sleep, the hush of blood
to the heart, a surge on a shore,
a slow breathing out, a letting go.

The length of the stroke is the scope
of an arm, the arc from the hip, the rise
and dip of your body as you move
the dirt of the living from courtyard

to corner: the sweepings, the cells
shed off human skin, animal hide,
ashes, stains, particles of panic,
night sweats, waking fears, the tears

of the world. In front of you
the dust of night appears
with its news of lost cities, fallen
statues, the moon. You bend in to it.

The motes hang together, caught up
in time, testing the borderline
between who they have been
and where they are going.

This broom, this body of twigs
slung together and tied with string,
sweeps the used days in its wake,
soughing away the regrets

of a lifetime. It strokes
the face of the earth and forgives
the waste. Everything
moves from dust to dust.
All that is lost
comes back as love.

Writing the Will

Before you begin to make an inventory
of material gains and worldly goods,
you are told it is possible and even advisable
to bequeath your entire digital history
to your heirs.

The horror of it. The ignominy.

She Is Trying On the Pre-loved Shoes

Parcels
are pouring in
from eBay
and from Amazon.
I've taught the dog
to sign for them
and take them in.
Sometimes
he buries them
in the back and that's
a relief because the binbags
are snarling at me
with eyes bulging
out of the corners
of every room.

What Bunny-Auntie Says to Bobby-Uncle

Now our pictures have been
photoshopped we do look
good together even if I say
so myself and there's the
proof popping up on the screen.
All that's missing is the poor
Yorkipoo and that would add
a thousand likes but he was
eaten by the vacuum cleaner
this morning and no one has
had time to empty the bag
to see if he's still there.

She Has an Off-day

Sod off if you've sold the book
or bagged the prize
or launched a career
or lost a stone
and dropped a dress size.
Sod off if you managed the holiday
in Sharm El Sheikh and posted
a picture of the swimming pool
and the strawberry Mojito
you are sipping this minute
with a pink umbrella and ice.

When I'm not like this I'm nice

really

(smiley face)

Bobby Saves Nature to the Cloud

I went for a walk and found some Nature.
Maybe it was a mouse or mole
or it could have been a rat

but it sort of looked at me like
What? So I took a photo,
got in the car and got the hell out

of the shithole
countryside and that
was that.

Auntie Death Says She Slays

Slick like molasses, trick you like sugar,
thick in your blood the morning after,

The salt on your chips, ghee in your paratha,
when you gorge on bread, I'll be the butter.

Have another lick. There's the kick of bliss.
When they told you about me, did you expect me
to be *this*?

Bubbles Experiences a Moment of Dread

Supposing
it comes back
into fashion
to bury the dead
with all they possess,
the laptops, phones,
chargers, computers,
flatscreens, consoles,
cupboards, sofas?
The shame of it,
the scale of the tomb
to be sunk underground
for the cars and hairdryers,
the unworn dresses
too tight to wear,
too dear to lose.
Think of the tons
of soil to be shovelled
out of the earth
for the shoes,
my god,
the shoes.

She Contemplates Her Death

Please don't write an obituary
or send a tweet that says
how sweet I was.

I died despising everything
and every one of you
and especially

did not appreciate the pictures
you hearted of rabbits
and donkeys.

Donor

Blue billows through the dancers
on a glassy stage

and lifts the offering
to the spotlight,

the alphabet of you
delivered to a waiting page

on cue.
Spin and turn

are choreographed to map
the body, who you were,

the cell, the single stroke
that carries your signature.

Lines meet and part
and meet again across a graph,

charting a course to unnamed stars.
The scientist scans the columns

and reads your promise
in numbers, paragraphs.

You are returned complete
and singular, no detail missed

under the eye that sorts and sifts
the dance of data from the gift.

Night Visitors

You can trust no one these days.

With daily muggings on the streets
and talk of burglaries, they call the experts in
to set up a network of interlocked alarms,
infrared cameras at the entry points, cunning
passwords, keys and fobs, sensors
that trigger alerts on multiple mobile phones.

They are reassured

all the things inside are secure, laptops,
consoles, golf clubs, miniatures,
the collection of samurai swords,
designer handbags, watches, rings.
Wherever they may be, New York, Abu Dhabi,
Beijing, they can watch the periphery.

They expect strangers

when the alerts begin. A fox skulks out of the bushes,
a squirrel steals down a tree, a rat squeezes through
a hole in the wall, all caught on camera. And here
is one who arrives in the night, not much more
than a breath spun into the lens, burnt out to white.
All systems switch on to watch it come,

an angel in a blur of light.

The Host

While I have been away the fruit flies
have moved in with their extended family
and rise politely off a feast of black
banana skin to welcome me home. I swat
and slap, but they just laugh on the updraft
of my flapping, batting hands.

The banana gone, I open a window, hoping
they will make off to some other repast
but they post a halo round my head,
two hundred wingbeats to a second, hatched
with a brain far quicker than mine. At my desk,
I am possessed, follow the threads for evidence

of pestilence, the death of civilisations
by Zebub, Arob, all the dust of Egypt
turned to gnats that torment livestock, squat
on ruined crop, rotted fish and frog.
In the face of this invasion, I am
an avenger sent to stop a plague,

enter *Kill Fruit Flies*, study the traps, fill
a glass jar with cider vinegar, stir in sugar,
cover with cunning cling-film, pierce and wait,
and they come, hover like decorous guests
at a table, perch on the rim. I watch them drown
one by one, then return to my desk. But just

as I begin to write, one rises up at the edge
of my sight like the crop-duster in *North
by Northwest*. I spin back into battle, set
the trap again, more delicious, more sugar, more
stealth. It sits on the lip, licks at the cling-film,
sips. I strike. It dies a vinegar death.

Through the rest of the day I revisit the site.
No sign of return. The next morning no one
is there, the jar untouched, my table bare
in the desolate kitchen. I try to work but keep
coming back to stand like an expectant host,
waiting to welcome the guest I miss.

The Guest

She ate alone for twenty-seven days
and found it pleasing,
the frugality of it.

On day twenty-eight
she put out the finest linen,
nine white plates, banks of glasses,
rounds of cheese, mounds of figs,
black grapes, blood oranges.
She opened the window
and invited you down
to her table. You came,
dressed as you always are
for a night on the town,
your fingers wrapped
round the stem of a glass,
egg moon, fish moon, moon
of the sprouting grass,
on your face the bloom of phlox.

You made no conversation
but sat there together,
the room breathing easy
around you,

unhooked from time.

Then you left,
the food untouched.

With empty hands

It's life that is the visitor, it comes and goes,
a guest with many faces.
It flickers for a second on the face of time
and brings no gifts for the host.

You write a window

This is how you labour through the night
at the kitchen table, tallying up again,
again, to get the merciless numbers right.
You weigh the loss against the gain,

the plumbing or the heating, the buzzing thing
that has to be plugged in to work, switched on
to keep the household running. You are writing
your life in figures. He is gone

and you are awake in the sonnet of a window,
the chiming of a house where children come
and stay. The paper blazes white. The shadow
at your shoulder knows your will. This room,

this page is the sum of all you have to say
and all you have to give, you give away.

Go to the child

The children are always ours

JAMES BALDWIN

Rise and go on a bitter night
when hope lies frozen in the ground,
hushed and hidden out of sight,
no living thing for miles around.

Even though the tears of the earth
have turned to crystal, rise.
Take the road that leads to a birth.
An infant calls and the heart replies.

See in the eyes a blazing star,
a spark of something newly born,
feet already walking on air,
holding a lifeline in the palm.

When at last you see the face
and feel on your cheek the baby's breath;
when you have known the grace
of a beginning, being blessed,

look up at the hungry bowl of the sky
and empty your pockets to fill it,
see where the water is rising
and lift your hands to still it,

turn to a world that is still unborn
and raise your voice to sing it,
go to the child who is not your own
and open your heart to save it.

See in the eyes a blazing star,
a spark of something newly born,
feet already walking on air,
holding a lifeline in the palm.

*

This is the embrace
that can heal and hold you safe.
Stranger, welcome home.

*

You are

You are the sound
that halts the breath.
You are the line
that has no stop,
the loop in time
that says time
is nothing.
You are the coin
that has two sides,
one that is owned
and one that is owed,
the unfinished ode,
the offered ring,
unsolved riddle,
unknown ratio.
You are the plate,
the brimming cup,
mouth of a bell,
the drop into a well
or tunnel that points
through darkness to light.
You are the moon,
the face in the night
that comes and goes,
wanes and grows
to zero. You multiply
to be yourself,
uncounted,
uncontained.

You are the death
where release begins,
a letting in, a letting go,
belly of earth,
door to birth.
You are in circling arms,
in hope, in song,
in the heart of now.
You are the end of no.

We are holding

We are holding each other
as if this is the last dance of the night,

the last song
before we lose the light.

Let's lie down here on the grass
and listen for whatever says goodnight.

But the radiance

But I didn't believe a word he said.
　　The Shadow Reader predicted
　　　　the year of my death, not how or where.
　　　　　　I shrugged and put it out of my head

but my body believed. There was no way I could die
　　at thirty-five or forty-five. I crossed murderous roads,
　　　　ran red lights in rickshaws, took flights
　　　　　　in turbulent skies, watched a plague go by

but in the Year of the Shadow, I remember the veins
　　on his hand, the finger he licked, the mark on the scroll.
　　　　I try to read the names of the ones who are dying
　　　　　　when it should have been me

but all I can see is the name of the earth, right here,
　　written over and over in the dying year.

*

We turn our faces up
to look for them, but the angels
are here, under our feet.

*

Your Session Has Been Terminated

He took my shadow like an unstitched
   length of cloth, washed the stories out and hung the rest
   to dry. What's left when the mess is rinsed away?

    Messages posted everywhere, parts of speech
    passers-by can only faintly hear, the best
    and least of what there is to say

      before the world shudders to a stop
      and the frozen frame becomes a shrine
      to what we were. Touched by god. Profane.

        We've lost you, you are breaking up.
        We'll come back to you when we have a better line.
        Try switching off and switching on again.

      It works sometimes.

Everywhere the angels

They are here with us, wings
thrust into silk and wool, crawling
over used surfaces where the body
has thrashed and turned and shed
its cells, its lovely dust.

They leave a trail of eggs that float
through warp and weft. The ghost
children will stay unnamed but eat
the beauty of this life till there is nothing
left of it but indrawn breath,

and they will find Jerusalem
in hair and fur, the fibre spun
from hope and dread
in a lifetime that will last days
and hang by a radiant thread.

I Walk in the Shadow

My walk is iambic. I keep the beat.
Shall I compare thee to ta*dum* ta*dum*?

There's comfort in knowing
that as long as the stress is in the right place

and as long as I keep up the pace
it doesn't matter where my feet are going.

If I can hear the iamb of my heart I'm not dead
yet. My walk is a sonnet.

My walk is *Ma Sha Allah*
My walk is *Fuck you, Shadow Reader.*

ACKNOWLEDGEMENTS

My thanks to *RA Magazine*, Royal Academy of Arts, Hew Locke, Imogen Greenhalgh and Sam Phillips; *Poetry London*, André Naffis-Sahely; *Wasafiri*, Susheila Nasta; *The Poetry Review*, Wayne Holloway-Smith; *Acumen*, Danielle Hope; *Write Where We Are Now*, Manchester Metropolitan University, Carol Ann Duffy; *Write Across London*, The Royal Society of Literature; *Sacred Sounds*, Alchemy, Nima Poovaya-Smith; *Furies: A Poetry Anthology of Women Warriors*, ed. Eve Lacey; *Anne-thology: Poems Re-presenting Anne Shakespeare* (Broken Sleep Books, 2023), ed. Paul Edmondson, Aaron Kent, Chris Laoutaris, Katherine Scheil; *Buzz Words: Poems About Insects* (Everyman's Library Pocket Poets Series, 2021), ed. Harold Schechter and Kimko Hahn; *Festival in a Book*, Liz Lefroy; The Royal Collection Trust, Emily Hannam; St Paul's Cathedral, Donna McDowell; The Manchester Poetry Library, Becky Swain; The Philip Larkin Society, Philip Pullen; Storyhouse Chester, Alex Clifton; Burg Hülshoff Center for Literature, Claudia Ehlert; Newcastle Centre for the Literary Arts (NCLA), Sinéad Morrissey; NCLA, Human Cell Atlas Project, Linda Anderson, Linda France, Kate Sweeney and Professor Muzlifah Haniffa, Medical Humanities Network, Newcastle University; BBC World Service, *Sweeping the World*, Emma-Louise Williams. Versions of these poems have previously appeared in *The Guardian* and been broadcast by the BBC. My special thanks to Neil Astley and everyone at Bloodaxe, for going above and beyond, always.